First World War
and Army of Occupation
War Diary
France, Belgium and Germany

4 DIVISION
12 Infantry Brigade
Royal Inniskilling Fusiliers
2nd Battalion
25 August 1914 - 31 December 1914

WO95/1505/2

The Naval & Military Press Ltd
www.nmarchive.com
Published in association with The National Archives

Published by

The Naval & Military Press Ltd

Unit 10 Ridgewood Industrial Park,

Uckfield, East Sussex,

TN22 5QE England

Tel: +44 (0) 1825 749494

www.naval-military-press.com

www.nmarchive.com

This diary has been reprinted in facsimile from the original. Any imperfections are inevitably reproduced and the quality may fall short of modern type and cartographic standards.

© Crown Copyright
Images reproduced by permission of The National Archives, London, England, 2015.

Contents

Document type	Place/Title	Date From	Date To
Heading	WO95/1505/2		
Heading	4th Division War Diaries 2nd Royal Innes. Hus August to December 1914 to 2 Div 5 Bde		
Heading	12th Brigade 4th Division 2nd Battalion The Royal Inniskilling Fusiliers August 1914		
Miscellaneous	The D.A.G. Gen H.Q. 3rd Echelon Nantes		
War Diary	Bertry	25/08/1914	25/08/1914
War Diary	Ligny	25/08/1914	25/08/1914
War Diary	Bevillers	25/08/1914	25/08/1914
War Diary	Esnes	26/08/1914	26/08/1914
War Diary	Ronssoy	26/08/1914	26/08/1914
War Diary	Le Catelet	26/08/1914	26/08/1914
War Diary	Hancourt	27/08/1914	27/08/1914
War Diary	Voyennes	28/08/1914	28/08/1914
War Diary	Campagne	29/08/1914	29/08/1914
War Diary	Troslybreuil	30/08/1914	30/08/1914
War Diary	Verberie	31/08/1914	31/08/1914
Heading	12th Brigade. 4th Division 2nd Battalion The Royal Inniskilling Fusiliers September 1914		
War Diary	Verberie	31/08/1914	31/08/1914
War Diary	Marchees From Verberie	01/09/1914	01/09/1914
War Diary	Barron	01/09/1914	02/09/1914
War Diary	Dan Martin	02/09/1914	03/09/1914
War Diary	Serris	04/09/1914	04/09/1914
War Diary	Jossigny	05/09/1914	05/09/1914
War Diary	Brie Comte Robert	06/09/1914	06/09/1914
War Diary	Villiers	07/09/1914	07/09/1914
War Diary	FM. Petit Loge	08/09/1914	08/09/1914
War Diary	Courcelles	08/09/1914	09/09/1914
War Diary	Les Boissieres	10/09/1914	10/09/1914
War Diary	Montigny (Cerfroid)	11/09/1914	11/09/1914
War Diary	Marizy-Simard	12/09/1914	12/09/1914
War Diary	Billy-Sur-Aisne	13/09/1914	13/09/1914
War Diary	Venizel	13/09/1914	13/09/1914
War Diary	St Marguerite	14/09/1914	30/10/1914
Heading	12th Brigade 4th Division 2nd Battalion Royal Inniskilling Fusiliers October 1914		
War Diary	Marguerite	01/10/1914	07/10/1914
War Diary	Septmonts	08/10/1914	08/10/1914
War Diary	Chacroise	09/10/1914	11/10/1914
War Diary	Longeuil	12/10/1914	13/10/1914
War Diary	Meterein	14/10/1914	14/10/1914
War Diary	Bailleul	15/10/1914	15/10/1914
War Diary	Ploegsteert	16/10/1914	17/10/1914
War Diary	Le Gheer	18/10/1914	18/10/1914
War Diary	Houplines	19/10/1914	19/10/1914
War Diary	Le Gheer	20/10/1914	21/10/1914
War Diary	Ploegsteert	22/10/1914	22/10/1914
War Diary	Armentieres	23/10/1914	29/10/1914
War Diary	Ploegsteert	30/10/1914	30/10/1914

War Diary	Messines	31/10/1914	31/10/1914
Miscellaneous	The Director, Historical Section, Military Branch, Committee Of Imperial Defence.	03/12/1923	03/12/1923
Miscellaneous	Statement by Captain & Brevet-Major C.A.M. Alexander, M.C., The Royal Inniskilling Fusiliers.	03/12/1923	03/12/1923
Heading	12th Brigade 4th Division. 2nd Battalion Royal Inniskilling Fusiliers November 1914		
War Diary	Messines	01/11/1914	07/11/1914
War Diary	Ploegsteert	08/11/1914	11/11/1914
War Diary	Le Bizet	12/11/1914	20/11/1914
War Diary	Nieppe	20/11/1914	26/11/1914
War Diary	Le Bizet	26/11/1914	30/11/1914
Miscellaneous	Strength Return.	02/12/1914	02/12/1914
Heading	12th Brigade 4th Division 2nd Battalion Royal Inniskilling Fusiliers December 1914		
War Diary	Le Bizet	01/12/1914	05/12/1914
War Diary	Bailleul	06/12/1914	06/12/1914
War Diary	Hazebrouck	07/12/1914	07/12/1914
War Diary	Wisques	08/12/1914	31/12/1914

warm 55 cm / 1505 (2)

warm 55 cm / 1505 (2)

4th Division
War Diary
2nd Royal Innis. Fus.

August to December
1914

To 2 DIV 5 BDE

12th Brigade.
4th Division.

2nd BATTALION

THE ROYAL INNISKILLING FUSILIERS

AUGUST 1 9 1 4.

The
D.A.G.
Gen. H.Q. 3rd Echelon
NANTES
~~~~~~~~~~

Herewith copy of War Diary for the period ending 31st August 1914.

We were under the impression that this had been already sent in.

Ca. Wilding, Major
Comdg 2/R Inniskilling Fusiliers

S⁺ MARGUERITE
25th Sept. 1914.

Army Form C. 2118

WAR DIARY
or
INTELLIGENCE SUMMARY.
(Erase heading not required.)

Instructions regarding War Diaries and Intelligence Summaries are contained in F. S. Regs., Part II. and the Staff Manual respectively. Title pages will be prepared in manuscript.

Hour, Date, Place	Summary of Events and Information	Remarks and references to Appendices
4.30 a.m. 25th Aug 14 BERTRY	Detrained	
6.30 a.m. 25 Aug 14 LIGNY	H.Qrs and two companies	
6.0 p.m. 25 Aug 14 BEVILLERS	2 companies. Engaged with small party Uhlans. 7.45 p.m.	
1.0 a.m. 26 Aug 14 ESNES	H.Qrs and two companies. Engaged with Enemy 8.5 am till 10.45 am and from 2.15 p.m. to 4.30 p.m.	
11.50 p.m. 26 Aug 14 RONSSOY	H.Qrs and two companies in retreat	
11.30 p.m. 26 Aug 14 LE CATELET	do	
	2 Companies do	
5.30 p.m. 27 Aug 14 HANCOURT	Battalion complete still in retreat left HANCOURT at 11.6 p.m.	
5.30 a.m. 28 Aug 14 MOYENNES	Halted ½ M. N. of MOYENNES sent back to MARTIGNY to cover retirement of 3rd Division across Sombre Canal at or near OFFOY — reached COMPAGNE 8 p.m.	
4 a.m. 29 Aug 14 COMPAGNE	marched to CHEVILLY stayed some hrs till 7 p.m. when march to NOYON commenced and continued marching all night until	
7 p.m. 30 Aug 14 TROSLY-BREUIL	reception of an hours halt at CHARLEPONT. Furnished night out posts started off at 5 p.m. arrived at VERBERIE 7 p.m. 31st Aug. 1914	
7 p.m. 31 Aug 14 VERBERIE		

A. Welding Major
Comdg 2nd Batt. Middlesex Regt

12th Brigade.
4th Division.

2nd BATTALION

THE ROYAL INNISKILLING FUSILIERS

SEPTEMBER 1 9 1 4

Army Form C. 2118.

WAR DIARY
or
INTELLIGENCE SUMMARY.

(Erase heading not required.)

September 1914

Instructions regarding War Diaries and Intelligence Summaries are contained in F.S. Regs., Part II. and the Staff Manual respectively. Title pages will be prepared in manuscript.

Hour, Date, Place	Summary of Events and Information	Remarks and References to Appendices
3pm. 31st Aug. VERBERIE	Arrived at VERBERIE – Took up Outpost position, facing N.W.	weather fine
4 am 1st Sept marched from VERBERIE.	Acting as rear guard – at dawn were attacked by Germans. They did not press the attack – managed to bring a M.G. into position & 6 Cyclists entering village – all killed. The enemy appeared to withdraw and move off round on left flank.	Casualties Officers: Capt. Robinson Lieut. Bradbull wounded Men 1 K. 24 W. 25 M.
3.30pm marched BARRON.		
12 midnight 1/2 Sept. BARRON	Moved off to escort ammunition Column	
11 a.m. 2nd Sept DAMMARTIN	Arrived at DAMMARTIN	
7 pm 3rd Sept "	Marched from DAMMARTIN to SERRIS	
5 pm 4th Sept SERRIS	Left SERRIS, after marching a few hours returned back to JESSIGNY	weather fine
12 m.n. 5th Sept JESSIGNY	Left JESSIGNY for BRIE COMTE ROBERT arriving there at 9 a.m.	
2 pm. 6th Sept BRIE COMTE ROBERT	Moved off to VILLIERS and there at an outpost line	
3.30 am 7th Sept VILLIERS	Stood to arms at 3 Be am. marched off at 12 noon to FERM PETIT LOGES beyond MAISONCELLES. While moving out to take up outpost position about 7 p.m. encountered party of enemy – Maxwell unknown who fired still fire.	Casualties Killed Lieut R A Floyd. wounded Capt V Hardey Men K. 1 W. 19 M. 6
5 am 8th FM PETIT LOGE.	Marched off at dawn and crossed the river PETIT MORIN at COURCELLES at 6 pm (2 Kil. E of LA FERTE). Germans were still seen in the village of COURCELLES as we approached.	weather fine

(9 29 6) W 3532—1107 100,000 10/13 H W V Forms/C. 2118/10.

WAR DIARY
or
INTELLIGENCE SUMMARY.
(Erase heading not required.)

Army Form C. 2118.

Instructions regarding War Diaries and Intelligence Summaries are contained in F. S. Regs., Part II. and the Staff Manual respectively. Title pages will be prepared in manuscript.

Hour, Date, Place	Summary of Events and Information	Remarks and References to Appendices
7 pm 8th Sep COURCELLES.	Put out outpost line to N.W. of COURCELLES and bivouacked on the road LA FERTE – BUSSIERES	Weather fine
5.30 am 9th "	Marched off as Rear Guard with orders to rise point 181 and then move to LES POUPS – and then to TARTARLL. Crossed the MARNE at SAUSSOY by railway bridge at 8 pm, and came under heavy shell fire close to the bridge (high explosives) No damage. Took up outpost line at LES BOISSIERES.	No casualties
5 am 10th LES BOISSIERES	Marched to MONTIGNY when ordered to put out outpost line. Found Uhlans had already done so – exchanged a few shots with them. Left spetsgon on both sides bivouacked for the night on the road MONTIGNY – CERFROID.	No casualties. Weather fine rather cold.
5.30 am 11th MONTIGNY. (CERFROID)	Marched to MARIZY-ST-HARD and billeted for the night.	Weather showery
5.20 am 12th MARIZY-S'HARD	Owing to a breakdown of Motor Cyclist Orderly – the march orders were lost in transmay so did not move off till nearly 9 am – marched to BILLY-SUR-AISNE via – CHOUY – HARTENNES – VILLEMONTOIRE – SEPTMONTS and billeted in BILLY-SUR-AISNE. 2 Coys on Outpost one of these Coys moved to the Bridge at VENIZEL – which had not been effectually blown up by the Germans – and caught a pinnace of the 4th Division trying to fix the charge again, the demolition was again unsuccessful.	Weather unsettled showery & cold. Heavy rain.

WAR DIARY or INTELLIGENCE SUMMARY

Army Form C. 2118.

Hour, Date, Place	Summary of Events and Information	Remarks and References to Appendices
6 am 13th Sept BILLY-SUR-AISNE	Moved to a Rdv 1K north of BILLY-SUR-AISNE, and then marched off to Vregny. Unsettled change of weather.	
2 pm	Heavy thunder and rain. Rest. High explosive fell in close proximity to the Battalion, no damage done to us — their shells appeared to come from the direction of CROUY.	No casualties
3 pm at VENIZEL	Proceeded to cross the AISNE and got safely over and under cover of the wood at M DES ROCHES — MISSY-SUR-AISNE. Heavily shelled in crossing from the west, and finally closed in Village of ST MARGUERITE. Enemy's gunfire coming from direction of VREGNY — CHIVRES	
(14th Sept to 30th Sept) ST MARGUERITE	Confusion. Took up a defensive position to the north and east of the village of ST MARGUERITE. CHIVRES strongly held by the enemy who are entrenched. Sniping prevalent and some men hit chiefly those in the neighbourhood of an extreme eastern position.	Officers W Lieut Eckhardt-Brown Men K 5 W 43 M 12
15th	Position same — Village shelled but little damage. Few casualties.	Officers W Steuer CE Dunlop K 1 Men W 9 M 1 Men W 3 M 4
16th	Position same. Hostile aeroplanes observed. A few shells.	
17th	do	
18th	do in attempt	Men W 2
22nd	Position same. Shelled daily and sniping continues.	Men W 3

Army Form C. 2118.

WAR DIARY
or
INTELLIGENCE SUMMARY.
(Erase heading not required.)

Instructions regarding War Diaries and Intelligence Summaries are contained in F. S. Regs., Part II. and the Staff Manual respectively. Title pages will be prepared in manuscript.

Hour, Date, Place	Summary of Events and Information	Remarks and References to Appendices
ST MARGUERITE. 23rd September	Position about the same — no signs of an attack being made by enemy.	Mem. w. 2
24th	— do — Several shells fell in village but away in direction of is difficult to drop shells into the village. The neighbouring villages of MISSY — CHIVRES — BUCY-LE-LONG have been shelled and are on fire. Enemy gunfire appears to come from the direction of PONT ROUGE — VREGNY — ORME. — The enemy artillery on the hill of CHIVRES appear to have been withdrawn owing to our artillery fire.	Mem. w. 1
25th – 30th Sept 29th Sept	Situation unchanged — sniping continues — own artillery duels daily.	Mem. w. 1

St Aignes Guérite
2 Oct. 14

R. Pratt Hylton(?) Major
Comdg. 3/A Army Billeting Division

W 3332–1107 103,000 10/13 H W V Forms/C. 2118/10.

12th Brigade.
4th Division.

2nd BATTALION

ROYAL INNISKILLING FUSILIERS

OCTOBER 1914

Army Form C. 2118.

WAR DIARY
or
INTELLIGENCE SUMMARY.
(Erase heading not required.)

2nd Battn. Royal Inniskilling Fusiliers.

Instructions regarding War Diaries and Intelligence Summaries are contained in F. S. Regs., Part II. and the Staff Manual respectively. Title pages will be prepared in manuscript.

Hour, Date, Place			Summary of Events and Information	Remarks and References to Appendices
1st Oct/14		St MARGUERITE.	Situation remains about the same. The Ridge to the north of Village very heavily shelled. No movement of the enemy observed. Sniping rather worse than usual.	Casualties W. 1 man. Weather very warm.
2nd "	6 am.	– do –	Situation same. 15th Bgd. withdrawn on our right and taken over by our troops 12 noon on. Sniper was captured by No. 10 Pdn. Batt. Hd. Qrs. moved to East end of St MARGUERITE. Shelled by Howitzers in the afternoon. Sniping prevalent.	Wounded from Artillery Concussion.
3rd "		– do –	Situation unchanged. Enemy artillery very quiet - our own artillery dittо. Sniping very much less.	K. 1 man. W. 1 man. Weather fine.
4th "		– do –	Situation unchanged. Enemy's Artillery more active. E. end of Village shelled. Capt Crawford + 1 man wounded. Sniping more quiet.	10 B K
5th "		– do –	Situation unchanged. Village shelled heavily but no casualties. Our Artillery shelled H.S. enemy in the afternoon and they then quiet.	
6th "		– do –	Situation unchanged. Very little shelling. Information that enemy strength to our front had been greatly reduced.	
7th "		do	Received orders to move to SEPTMONTS. Transport left at 4 p.m. The Battn. withdrew at 1.15 a.m. marched to the AISNE and crossed by	
	5 p.m.		pontoon bridge arrived at SEPTMONTS at 6 a.m. and billeted. Battn. went by Route March to VILLEMONTOIRE 6 - 8 p.m.	
8th "		SEPTMONTS.	Received orders to move to CHACROISE at 2 p.m. arrived at 4.30 p.m. and went into billets.	
9th "		CHACROISE.	Bn. went on Route March and Exercises on ground between CHACRISE and DROIZY 10 a.m. to 1 p.m. Received orders for all Transport & horses to move to LONGEUIL. Transport moved off at 6.30 p.m.	
10th "		– do –	Bn. went on Route March and Exercises 1 - 4.30 p.m.	
11th "		– do –	Battn. preceded by Motor Vans to LONGEUIL and billeted.	
12th "		LONGEUIL.	Battn. commenced entraining at 4 a.m. and moved off at 8.30 a.m.	
13th "			Train arrived at 2 a.m. Battn. commenced to dis-entrain at 5.30 a.m. and moved into billets. Heavy firing heard to S.E. Marched from billets at 10.50 a.m. and came in contact with enemy about 3 p.m. on the	

WAR DIARY or INTELLIGENCE SUMMARY.

Army Form C. 2118.

Hour, Date, Place		Summary of Events and Information	Remarks and References to Appendices
13th Oct. (continued)	METEREN	in the neighbourhood of METEREN, fierce fighting. Village taken during the night. One Officer killed & 4 men, Major Layne wounded, 7 men killed & 18 wounded.	Heavy rain during afternoon.
14th "	METEREN	Hardly opposed in our further advance through village. Casualties amounted to 1 Offr. and 1 man wounded. Consequent upon the falling back to the north, Batt. moved at 5 p.m. and arrived at BAILLEUL at 9 p.m. Billeted.	
15th "	BAILLEUL	Received orders to move at 6 a.m. Halted for the night at 8 p.m. Bivouacked.	
16th "	PLOEGSTEERT	Ordered to march about 9 a.m. to PLOEGSTEERT, which we reached just before dusk, and out of another field we entered, found two troops of cavalry brigade, and out of the fields cut out on the other side entered facing East. A reconnaissance of skirmishing of the Cavalry patrols during the afternoon which died away towards nightfall.	
17th "	PLOEGSTEERT	The enemy's patrols advanced along the river. Heavy artillery fire N. East of our position from 2 a.m. to 3.30 a.m. Received orders to move forward to LE GHEER and to keep position — line just East of village facing PONTROUGE, passed a quiet night.	
18th "	LE GHEER	Several pushes forward supported by Artillery. 10 to night a demonstration against PONTROUGE. The village was very heavily shelled & the Cavalry Brigade suffered very severely. In the evening the Batt. was ordered to HOUPLINES.	
19th "	HOUPLINES	Arrived at HOUPLINES at 8 a.m. Billeted. Orders to return to LE GHEER	
20th "	LE GHEER	Enemy attacked our position at 7 a.m., continued up to about 11 a.m. at which time we	
21st "	— do —	our advanced posts were driven in. Casualties 6 men killed, 16 wounded. General attack on our lines was unsuccessful. We were driven back & ordered to retire to our forward trenches. Returned to billets in PLOEGSTEERT at 10 p.m. Came thro' Capt. R. C. Macdonald, Capt. J. G. Pat. V and Lieut. M. Roberts killed and Lieut. J. W. Williams & 2nd Lieut. A. C. Bryon wounded. 33 men killed & 78 wounded. 12 missing.	
22nd "	PLOEGSTEERT	Billeted in PLOEGSTEERT.	
23rd "	ARMENTIÈRES	Ordered to ARMENTIÈRES.	
24th "	— do —	at ARMENTIÈRES.	

Army Form C. 2118.

WAR DIARY
or
INTELLIGENCE SUMMARY.
(Erase heading not required.)

Instructions regarding War Diaries and Intelligence Summaries are contained in F. S. Regs., Part II. and the Staff Manual respectively. Title pages will be prepared in manuscript.

Hour, Date, Place	Summary of Events and Information	Remarks and References to Appendices
25th Oct. ARMENTIERES.	At ARMENTIERES.	
26th " " do "	" do "	
27th " " do "	Were attacked in the morning by the enemy who were repulsed after obstinate fighting leaving several dead on the ground. Our losses were 1 killed and 15 wounded.	
28th " " do "	In trenches.	
29th " " do "	Billetted in ARMENTIERES.	
30th " PLOEGSTEERT	Went to PLOEGSTEERT and one company to HESSINES.	
31st " HESSINES	Heavy fighting at HESSINES lot recaptured. Several trenches from the Germans which trenches had been taken from the 55th Rifles the previous day. Our Casualties 2/Lt Brennan Touche serverely wounded Captain Adj! Reg Bald slightly wounded 9 killed 18 wounded	

31st October 1914.

C. A. Wilding
Lieut. Colonel,
Commanding 2nd Bn. Royal Irish Rifle Fusiliers.

ORDERLY ROOM
No. 1009
3 DEC 1923
DEPOT
R. INNISKILLING FUSILIERS
OMAGH.

The Director,

  Historical Section, Military Branch,

    Committee of Imperial Defence.

....

    With reference to your No. H/2., dated 29th November, 1923.

    I forward herewith statement by Captain & Bt. Major C. A. M. Alexander, M.C., who was serving with the 2nd Battalion, The Royal Inniskilling Fusiliers, on 1st November, 1914.

    Map is returned herewith.

                Captain,

  Commanding Depot, The Royal Inniskilling Fusiliers.

Omagh, 3rd December, 1923.

Statement by Captain & Brevet-Major C.A.M.Alexander, M.C.,
The Royal Inniskilling Fusiliers.

....

On the 31st October, 1914, the Company to which I belonged - "A" Company, 2nd Bn., The Royal Inniskilling Fusiliers - relieved Indian Troops in the front line. Three Platoons were in the line and the remaning Platoon and Company Headquarters were in support near Battalion Headquarters, which was on the PLOEGSTEERT - MESSINES Road, about 400 yards in rear of the line. "B" Company was on our left and was the extreme left Company of the 4th Division. The River Douve was the right of "A" Company Sector. "D" Company was South of the River Douve - "A" Company Patrols visited DOUVE FM on night October 31st/1st November, - it was unoccupied.

On the morning of November 1st, I saw troops of the Division on our left withdrawing from MESSINES. They did so without giving my Battalion any warning. The flank of the 4th Division then became exposed, and, I understand, my Battalion received orders to withdraw to the 2nd line and to cover Hill 63.

Our trenches were shallow and wet - the line was disconnected. Each section of trench would accommodate a platoon (about 15 men) and there was one hundred yards between platoons. Messengers sent from Company Headquarters with orders for the withdrawal were hit, but one message reached 2/Lieutenant K. S. Alpin, who was commanding the right platoon of "A" Company. This platoon was to pass on the message to the Platoon on its left, which I commanded. I saw Lieutenant K. S. Alpin get out of his trench also one man - both were instantly killed. The Non-commissioned Officer in charge did not make further effort to pass on the message but held on to his trench. The ground was overlooked by the enemy and any movement by us drew fire. All day we saw the enemy massed on the Ridge and advancing towards our line. I decided that we must endeavour to deceive them as to our strength and having a good supply of S. A. A. bursts of rapid fire were kept up throughout the day. The rifles of casualties also being used. I think the enemy were uncertain as to our position - I know they had many casualties and did not press their attack that day. DOUVE FM was heavily shelled by the enemy. At dusk, as neither "A" nor "B" Companies had reported to Battalion Headquarters, a patrol under O. C. "A" Company was sent out to clear up the situation. The patrol were @@@@@@@ surprised to find that the two Companies were still in their position and had not been surrounded. Practically all ammunition had been expended. Under cover of darkness we collected our casualties and withdrew.

                                          Captain (Bt. Major).,
                          The Royal Inniskilling Fusiliers.
Omagh, 3rd December, 1923.

12th Brigade.
4th Division.

2nd BATTALION

ROYAL INNISKILLING FUSILIERS

NOVEMBER 1 9 1 4

Army Form C. 2118.

WAR DIARY
or
INTELLIGENCE SUMMARY.

(Erase heading not required.)   2nd Royal Inniskilling Fusiliers

Instructions regarding War Diaries and Intelligence Summaries are contained in F. S. Regs., Part II. and the Staff Manual respectively. Title pages will be prepared in manuscript.

Hour, Date, Place	Summary of Events and Information	Remarks and references to Appendices
1914 November 1 MESSINES.	Holding line of forward trenches. Regiments on our left flank retired without giving us warning. Held the trenches till nightfall when we retired to second line of trenches about one mile. By casualties - 2nd Lieut K. S. Aplin and four men killed; Major R.G. Pierce & 22 men wounded. 6 men missing. Remained in trenches.	
" 2 -do-	-do- -do- Coming back into supporting trenches in the wg.	
" 3 -do-	-do- -do- 1 man missing.	
" 4 -do-	Casualties - 4 men wounded. One coy. sent out to support French attack. Still in Reserve trenches.	10
" 5 -do-	Still in Reserve. Whole Regiment called out to support the Dorsets which aids not come off.	
" 6 -do-	Still in Reserve. Whole Regiment called out to support the Dorsets who thought they were being attacked.	
" 7 -do-	Still in Reserve. Went out in morning to recover trenches on edge of PLOEGSTEERT Wood. Two desperate assaults were made led by Capt H.R.G. Spearn, on the trenches which the Germans had taken from the Wiltshire Regt. We were unfortunately repulsed with heavy casualties. Lieut. J.R. Bingham & 9 men killed. Lieut Loram & 2nd Lieut J.R. Ludlow and 64 men wounded. 2nd Lieut S.B.Duff slightly wounded. A.J.L. Barton wounded & missing. 16 men missing. Lieut S.B.Duff slightly wounded. Held on to edge of wood all day. Returned to billets in PLOEGSTEERT during the night.	
" 8 PLOEGSTEERT.	Returned to Support and Reserve trenches in PLOEGSTEERT Wood. Remained in these trenches and assisted in an attack on three trenches which we had previously attacked on 7th Nov. Captain Steward volunteered to make a further trenches attack on these trenches but the 1st. Argyll & Sutherland Highlanders considered that sufficient loss had already been incurred and declined to co-operate. Casualties - Capt. B. Hanly Wounded. 2 men killed. 2 men wounded.	
" 9 —"—		
" 10 —"—		

Army Form C. 2118.

WAR DIARY
or
INTELLIGENCE SUMMARY.
(Erase heading not required.)

Instructions regarding War Diaries and Intelligence Summaries are contained in F. S. Regs, Part II. and the Staff Manual respectively. Title pages will be prepared in manuscript.

Hour, Date, Place		Summary of Events and Information	Remarks and references to Appendices
November 11	PLOEGSTEERT	Remained in trenches in PLOEGSTEERT Woods. About 8 A.m. received orders to proceed to LE BIZET and take over some trenches in support of Kings Own, with two Companies.	
12.	LE BIZET.	At 10 A.m. my other two Companies having been relieved by Rifle Brigade marched to LE BIZET. Two Companies were ordered to take over part of the Kings Own line from the LE TOQUET Rly to the X roads quarter mile S.E. of E.II WARNAVE connecting with 1st Hampshires. The other two Coys and H.Q. were billeted in LE BIZET	
13—20	LE BIZET	Battns. H.Q. and men billeted in LE BIZET. No change in situation of Battalion. The two Companies in front were relieved every second night by the other two Companies.	Some shell and rifle fire.
20	NIEPPE	Battalion were ordered to NIEPPE to allow the men to have a bath and change of clothing.	Weather continuously wet
21	do	Bath when had, to together a change of clothing the Battn. then proceeded to new billets in NIEPPE.	— do —
22.	do	Lieut Col. R. A. Wilding proceeded on short leave to England.	
23. 24	do	Battn. remained in billets in NIEPPE. Two Coys were engaged daily with the R.E. in digging trenches. The others were compelled to find starting parties on the pontoons at B. 40	Weather continued frosty till 24th when came on rain fall.
25	LE BIZET	Battn returned to former billets in LE BIZET. One Coy was detached as flying picquet under the name of White Coy in reserve.	
26	— do —	From 24th engaged in support trenches two Coys with R.E. & two with Kings Own.	
28	— do —	First Coat & Mackintosh allotted to take part in attack of Battn., and accounts temporary composed of 1st & 2nd Bns.	108
29—30	— do —	Battn. in fragments in support trenches, other than the front line.	

30th Nov, 1914

E.A.H. Newman Capt

for Lieut Colonel

Commanding 2nd Bn R. Inniskilling Fus.

STRENGTH RETURN.

Detail.		Officers Number.	Other ranks Number.	Remarks.
Strength of Unit on 30th Nov. 1914.		18	902	Includes draft of 4 Offrs & 188 Other ranks joined 12 M.N. 30-11-14 Am. Sgt at Sleenwrench
Details, by arms attached to unit as in War establishment	A.S.C. R.A.M.C. etc.	1	3	
	A.O.C.		1.?.	
Total		19	906	

Signature _____

Unit _____ R. Innis Yes

Date

/12/1914.

URGENT.

This return to be completed and forwarded through the usual channel to reach Div. H.Q.'s by 12 M.D. on 3rd Dec. 1914.

2/12/14.

(Sd) J. Smyth Colonel
Lt. Col.
A.A. & Q.M.G. 4th Div.

12th Brigade.
4th Division.

2nd BATTALION

ROYAL INNISKILLING FUSILIERS

DECEMBER 1 9 1 4

2nd Royal Inniskilling Fusiliers

Army Form C. 2118.

WAR DIARY
or
INTELLIGENCE SUMMARY.
(Erase heading not required.)

Instructions regarding War Diaries and Intelligence Summaries are contained in F. S. Regs., Part II. and the Staff Manual respectively. Title pages will be prepared in manuscript.

Hour, Date, Place	Summary of Events and Information	Remarks and references to Appendices
1914.		
Dec. 1st to 5th, LE BIZET	Battalion remained in billets and was engaged in digging trenches in the front line. Lieut. Col. G.C. Wilding rejoined from leave on 1st Dec.	
Dec. 6th, BAILLEUL	Ordered to join Brigade Reserve at WISQUES, near ST. OMER. To refit. Marched to BAILLEUL and billetted.	
" 7th, HAZEBROUCK	Marched to HAZEBROUCK and billetted.	
" 8th, WISQUES	Marched to WISQUES, via ST. OMER, and billetted in convent.	
" 8th - 31st, WISQUES	Remained in Brigade Reserve and refitted. Strength of Battalion on 30th November, 12 Officers, 742 other ranks. " " " " 31st December 28 " 995 " "	

31st Dec. 1914.

C.A. Wilding Lieut. Colonel.
Commanding 2nd Royal Inniskilling Fus.

www.ingramcontent.com/pod-product-compliance
Lightning Source LLC
Chambersburg PA
CBHW081506160426
43193CB00014B/2608